TO THE YOUNGER

Stories and Lessons to Help Teenagers and Young Adults Deal With Life's Problems and See the Big Picture

(Self Esteem, Substance Abuse, Depression, Suicidal Thoughts, Bullying and Judging Others, Losing Love, and Making Good Choices to Help You Live a Happy Life)

By Mark J. Spanbauer
Photographs by Amanda J. Spanbauer

To The Younger
Written by Mark Spanbauer
Edited by Griffin Mill
Layout & Design by Michael Nicloy
Cover & Interior Photographs by Amanda J. Spanbauer

ISBN: 978-1945907333

Published by Nico 11 Publishing & Design
www.nico11publishing.com

Be well read.

Quantity purchase requests can be emailed to:
mike@nico11publishing.com

FOREWORD

The purpose of this book is to try to help teenagers and young adults deal with the difficulties young people face throughout their early years. Looking at the big picture can be difficult to do when one is having problems with issues such as low self-esteem, substance abuse, depression, suicidal thoughts, being bullied or judged by others, losing love or lack of love, lack of athletic ability, fitting in, and other problems young people face growing up in these difficult times. Learning how to overcome the problems you have as you make your way through life is very important.

Everyone is different, which is what makes us all unique and valuable. Please understand that there is a place for you and everyone in this world; everyone just has to find their niche. Making proper choices when you are having problems is the key to working through your problems, and moving on to a happy and meaningful life.

Talking to a counselor or other professional, or to a trusted adult, is important so you can get the proper help you need. Calling 911 for help in extreme cases is not a sign of weakness, but actually a sign of strength. Trying to mask your problems by abusing substances only leads to more problems, and makes things worse.

I hope the stories and lessons in this book help you to open your eyes so you see the big picture. As you will read in this book, there are many young people who never got the chance that you now have in front of you; the chance for a long and meaningful life if you make the right choices.

Good luck.

To the Younger

I want to help and I know it's hard
For you to see things the way I do.
But believe it or not, there was a time
When I was young and I had troubles too.

The young life I knew was not like yours
More difficult times now, I have to admit.
But you and I have some common things too
Over the years I have learned quite a bit.

We also had bullies, there were drugs and alcohol,
Our life back then not just a stroll in the sun.
We had to study and we had to work,
So don't think times back then were all fun.

There were days when I also got overwhelmed,
A few times thought that I'd reached the end.
But thank God that I never took that last step,
And because I didn't now please understand.

If you get to the point where you want to give up,
There are people who want to help you,
All you have to do is go ask for some help.
Take that step they will help you get through.

As time goes on you'll see things differently
You will be happy with the choice that you made.
The tough times will fade and you'll realize
You are happy you chose life and you stayed.

Please understand that you are not alone and that many people have had some of the problems that you are feeling. If you are having trouble with any aspect of your life, please talk to someone (Counselor, Other Professional, Trusted Adult, and in extreme cases, please call 911). There are people that can help you get through what you are going through.

If Only

I didn't take my walk that day,
But when I do I usually go that way.
If I'd only bundled up and gone
I might have stopped something so wrong.

I might have met her on her way
To take that jump to go away.
That might have made her think a bit,
She might have changed her mind walked away from it.

Or I might have seen her standing there,
Upon the edge might have caught her stare.
Maybe we'd have talked and I'd have helped her to see...
Helped to calm her stress, and maybe set her free.

Or even if I'd just heard her cry
Down in the icy water as I walked on by.
Then I maybe could have jumped and tried
To save that sweet girl before she died.

Because it wasn't time for her to go,
She was too young and didn't know
How to handle those who didn't see
Her inner beauty and just let her be.

Please God, don't blame her for what she did.
She was so young, such knowledge hid.
She was pushed too far and didn't know...
So in her mind she had to go.

A very sad time in my life, and a reason I started this book; to try to help young people think things through and make good choices. Get help if you are hurting or something is bothering you. Call 911 if you feel like you are reaching the end; people are here to help you.

Never a Mom

She never became a mother to a daughter or a son,
She never felt the beauty of being needed by someone,
To hear them cry and calm them and to hold them close to her,
To smell the freshness of their skin she missed it all for sure.

What mattered to her was that next good high.
Go and catch that really great buzz
That mattered more, you wonder why.
All you can say it was so just because.

She'll never take those buggy walks,
One of the greatest joys of all.
Never rake a great big pile of leaves,
Jump in and hide with her kids during fall.

Or build a snow fort with them so fun
When the snow is so packy and just right.
Read a book to them and watch them fall asleep,
Warm and safe in their bed every night.

She never got to do those things.
Her days wasted, it just doesn't seem right
That last great buzz ruined everything for her,
Because it ended her life late one night.

Far too many beautiful young ladies die because of drug abuse, suicide, and other causes; before they even get to experience some of the great joys of life. Please make good choices so you hopefully get the chance to live a long and happy life.

It's OK

It's OK for you to admit
That there's something that's bothering you.
You are not weak, I hope you see
That it's a strong thing when you do.

We all have our flaws inside and out,
Some are seen others are hidden inside.
To admit that we hurt there's nothing wrong
So just do it and swallow your pride

Please ask for help, there is no shame.
Lots of people do it every day.
It's OK to admit that you have pain,
And then you can be on your way.

To finding that there's another way,
Yes, you have flaws but you are so much more.
Please ask for help to help you to see
Life can be good when you open that door.

Everyone has troubles at some time in life and there is no shame to ask for help if you need it. Talking to a counselor, other professional, a trusted adult, or calling 911 in extreme cases, is what you should do if you need help.

A Parent's Nightmare

Fast asleep suddenly jolted awake
A phone call came to them late that night
Both of them fearfully sensed right away
They knew something just must not be right.

And the caller on the other end
His words changed their world for sure
He told them that the one they loved
Was all gone was all gone forever more.

Just a bunch of kids they got into that car
Never dreamed that it would not end right
Laughing and drinking their car missed that curve
They all died on that terrible night.

And the parents' lives changed right there
They had loved that child since they were born
When they got that news that their loved one was gone
Out of their chests then their hearts had been torn.

Drinking and driving; imagine how your parents, brothers, sisters, friends, relatives, etc., would feel if this happened to you.

Before

Please think about your family.
Please think about your friends.
Just think what it will do to them,
Just imagine if your life ends.

Please think beyond the moment,
That is all I'm asking of you.
Please think beyond the moment
Before that needle goes into you.

There are other paths that you can take.
Yes you can choose another way.
There are other plans that you can make,
To make sure you live beyond today.

Your family and friends, they need you.
Please stop and think that through.
They love you, I know you know it's true.
Without you here, what would they do?

If you are shooting up, you need to stop before it's too late and get help right away. Please call 911 and tell them that you need help; they will get you the help you need.

Big Man

6 by 8 cell day after day.
For seven long years it will be that way.
Just because you had to be a big man,
Except this part wasn't in your plan.

Each day you stare at those dull, drab walls.
The same routine up and down the same halls
Like a caged dog just trying to survive.
You worry that you won't make it out alive.

Because you got those drugs for her,
Never thinking such a bad thing could occur.
But she died so young - yes, what a shame.
And you got them for her, so you are to blame.

And though someday you'll get out of there,
There's something forever that will be true,
Each year on that date you'll always know
That she died because of you.

If you are supplying drugs for others, this may happen to someone and their life will end; and your life will be changed forever.

Just A Couple Buddies

They were just a couple buddies
And they liked to goof around,
Party all night go out on the town,
Find mischief where it could be found.

But one night they went a bit too far
Trying to reach that ultimate high.
Took too many pills and went to sleep.
To their family and friends, no goodbye.

They thought that they were invincible,
Push the limit and still be around.
But that night those buddies ran out of luck,
And the Oxy took them down.

Family and friends are left to deal
That those guys are no longer here.
Just a couple of buddies who ran out of luck,
Put into the ground because they had no fear.

A sad story about two guys from my home town.
They did illegal drugs one night, and ended up dying.

My Old Friend

Said goodbye to My Old Friend yesterday,
Always there for me I could count on it.
Ever since I can remember My Old Friend's been there,
Through thick and thin brought me courage and wit.

Countless times I've tried to tell it goodbye.
Somehow My Old Friend always came back to me
Like a crutch to help me hobble through life
Blinded my eyes I was not able to see.

Despite all the good times My Old Friend showed me
In reality way much more trouble instead.
When I'm honest and look in the mirror I say
That I wish that My Old Friend was dead.

But I'm smart enough since I've tried it before.
My Old Friend lurks and it's never too far.
All I have to do is walk in through that door,
My Old Friend's waiting for me at the bar.

This is about my personal fight with alcohol; but this also applies to any addiction. Total abstinence is the only surefire way for staying free from any substance abuse.

Wild Flower

Wild Flower she was so beautiful and free,
Could grow and be what she wanted to be.
An endless smile she was loved by all,
But slowly the poison came and took it all.

That beautiful flower so young and free,
Why she ruined her life, how could it be?
Sneaked in on her and took her away.
Wild Flower so beautiful started wilting one day.

Everything she was and all that she had,
Wild Flower was lost beyond so sad.
The drugs took her, she did not stay.
Now that beautiful flower has gone away.

Missed out on the good things her life could be,
The drugs took it all and she couldn't see.
Beautiful Wild Flower she had so much ahead,
Wild Flower was poisoned, she wound up dead.

To see young people fade away and finally die because of drug addiction is a terrible thing. If you see yourself trapped in addiction, please call 911 and they will get you to people that will help you.

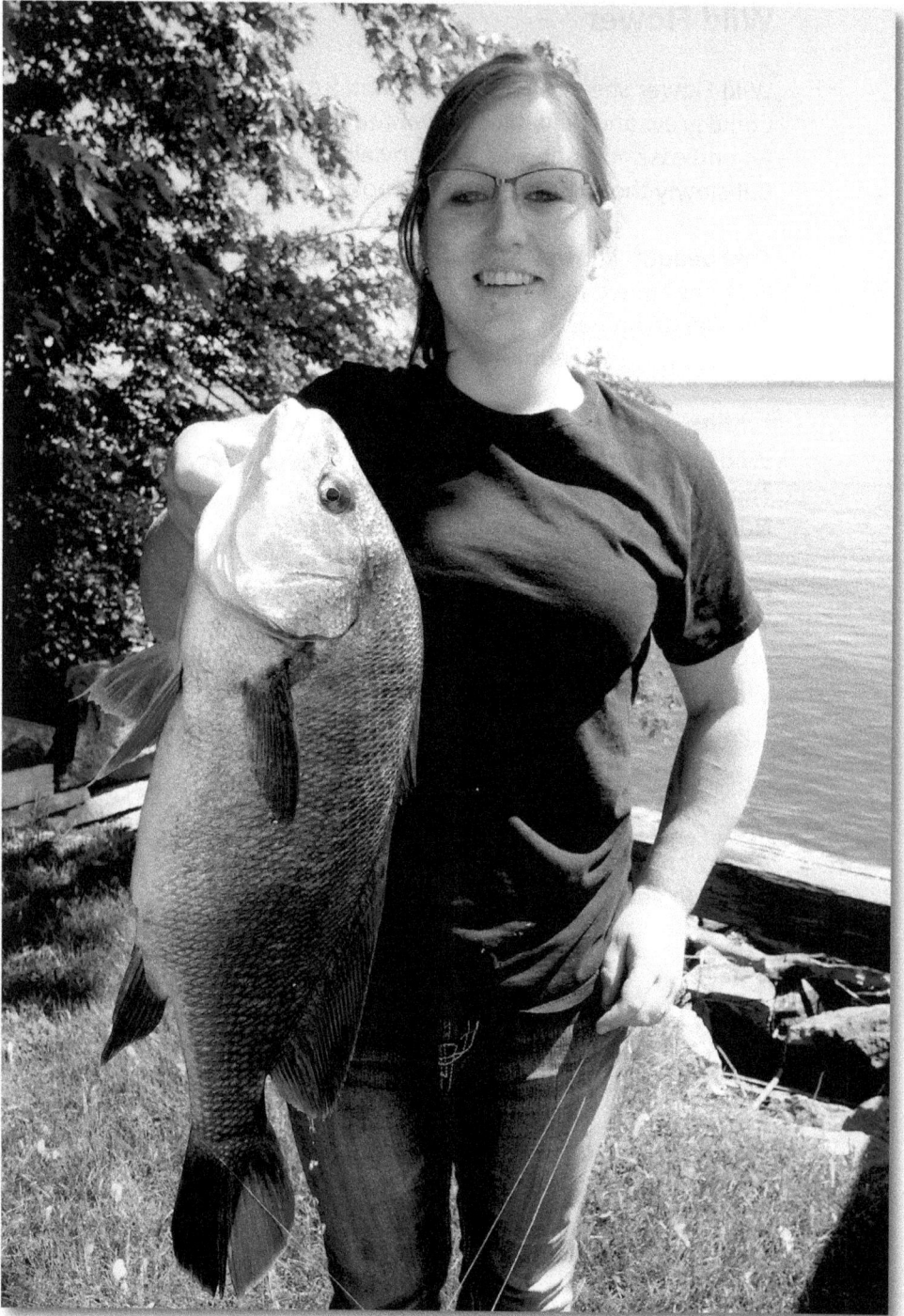

Don't Worry

You are young and everything seems pretty bad,
All you hear on the news is doom and gloom.
They rarely speak of the good mostly the sad,
Sometimes you just want to stay inside your room.

Please don't worry, don't be sad, it's not the end.
There's way more good in this world, believe me.
When I write to you all I'm trying to send
Is a message to ease your mind so you see.

There are so many nice people that are out there.
Much more good than all the bad stuff that you hear.
Many more people doing good things they do care,
So please stop worrying don't listen to the fear.

Live your life look at the beauty that surrounds you,
Look for the good open your eyes and you will see
Many good people and the good things that they do.
See through the bad and much happier you will be.

For some reason the news outlets (television, newspapers, internet, etc.) mainly concentrate on reporting the bad things that happen in the world. There is much more good in the world than bad; all you have to do is look for it.

Please Think

Although you aren't my daughter,
Although you aren't my son,
Please think about how they would feel
Since you are their special one.

Because I do not even know you
But it would break my heart in two.
No I do not even know you,
But I'd be in mourning over you

Before you do that thing you plan to do,
I just want you to think and to see
What it would do to those that love you.
If you were mine what it would do to me.

Please think about how they would feel
If you did something that is so wrong.
What it would do to those that love you
When that special part of their heart is all gone.

If you have thoughts of doing something harmful to yourself, please talk to a counselor or other trusted adult right away, or call 911. People are there for you and can get the proper help for you right away.

Your Picture

I saw your picture in the paper today,
It's been a year since you went away
From mom and dad and those that loved you.
A memorial of love, what else can they do?

Always in their hearts, always on their minds,
Memories of them and you and much happier times.
If you could only see what it's done to them,
You might have changed some things back then.

Because on that day that you gave up hope,
In your mind you had reached the end of your rope.
Not only did you put an end to your life,
You also changed forever your father and his wife.

If you only would have tried to talk to someone
Something for you then could have been done.
You'd be here, and your mom and dad you'd see,
At the end of their lives, they could have died happily.

*For the sake of all the people that love you, please get some help
before you do something that will hurt so many people forever.
Call 911 or the Suicide Hotline if you are having problems.*

Day by Day

Then it all came tumbling down that year
Nowhere to run nowhere to hide for me
Panic set in and suddenly nothing was clear
More than I could handle then it seemed to be

Thought I was doing OK and everything was good
Affairs in order doing the things I thought were right
But the wall crashed down would change things if I could
Got so much harder to get a good sleep every night

Overwhelmed so much at once the pressure took its toll
End of the rope the stress too much and I couldn't see
The toughest part was that I didn't seem to have control
Those things inside so strong had control of me

Then one night it came to me "don't let all this stuff bother you"
"What good is that? You have to take things one by one"
"Take some deep breaths and the fresh air will show you what to do"
And in a while my darkness replaced by the morning sun

Where did they come from those words that helped me through?
I'd like to say that I don't know but I'd be lying
The words I heard without a doubt they came from you
Hard to explain some time ago I just quit trying

Why should we worry, what good is it, when we know it's so
Can't speed up time to make our troubles go away
Slow things down and one by one away each problem will go
Things will get better if we just take things day by day

If things in life pile up on you and you start to feel overwhelmed, make a list and address each problem one by one. If you start with the most serious problem and work your way down your list then day by day things will get better as time goes by.

Who Made You Judge?

Some people call them misfits,
And some people call them weird,
Some people ridicule and hate them,
And some people call them queers.

Because they see life in a different way,
The so-called "normal" put them down.
Because they're different people call them gay,
The so-called "normal" does not want them around.

From what I have seen they all have a heart.
Open your eyes is what you have to do.
From what I've seen no don't even start
To say that they're not as good as you.

What gives you the right to judge someone
Just because they are different than you?
To judge someone's daughter or someone's son,
Just because they don't see things like you.

People are born the way they are; it's all genetics, so you are what you are. Just because someone doesn't look like you or think like you doesn't give you the right to make fun of them or ridicule them.

Fun and Games?

It started out as fun and games,
She was an easy target to attack.
They never said things to her face
They always said stuff behind her back.

But like they do, those words did get out.
She wasn't stupid, she could hear and could see.
And at night when she tried to go to sleep
She lay awake always thinking "why me?"

What did I ever do to them?
I'm not cool, I stay out of their way.
I'm not very pretty, I'm not very smart,
And sometimes I don't know what to say.

But their fun and games went on and on,
She felt alone always hiding her pain.
So one night as she lay hopeless and alone
Her light went out, she extinguished her flame.

Making fun of others, either in front of them or behind their backs, is a terrible thing to do; and far more hurtful than you realize. How would you feel if you were the one that the others were making fun of?

Why?

Why did you all gang up on her?
To bring yourself up or to take her down?
Did it make you happy did it make you smile
To watch that poor girl sit and frown?

If the shoe were on the other foot
And you were her and she were you
How would you feel to be in her place?
Would you want them to do that to you?

You really don't have to follow the crowd
When things are done that you know aren't right.
You can put your foot down and say that it's wrong,
I guarantee that you'll sleep better at night

And true friends will follow you and respect you,
The phony ones will fade away and you'll see,
Because deep down you did what you know is right.
Much better friends and much happier you'll be.

Be a leader and stand up for what you know is right and be against what you know is wrong. It is the right thing to do and you and your friends will be a much happier because of it.

Skin Deep

When you look into the mirror
Don't judge yourself by what you see
There's more to you than meets the eye.
I'm just like you so you can trust me.

There's much more to life than just your looks,
At your age I know it's hard for you to see.
But like a book you can't just judge the cover,
It's what's inside that will help you to achieve.

There are many things that you can do with your life
To make a difference before you are through.
When you help someone do you think they care?
About your looks, no it's your kindness that makes you.

So try to remember this thing I say.
I'm just like you so you can trust me.
Your true beauty lies within yourself,
Not the face in the mirror that you see.

Not everyone is blessed with beauty or good looks. Being a nice person who is good to others is so much more important. Beauty and good looks fade away; being kind and helping others, or even helping animals, never grows old.

Just Different

He wasn't born a macho guy,
And you know there is no reason why.
But just because he's not like you
Is that a reason to harass him like you do?

If you don't like him, just let him be.
He's no threat to you, surely you can see.
Does it make you manly does it make you cool?
Maybe you think so, but to most you're a fool.

He goes through his life day after day
Not bothering others he stays out of the way.
The feelings he has hidden deep inside,
He knows he is different that he can't hide.

Yes he's a bit different but he's got feelings too.
Beyond his looks not much different than you.
He has needs and wants to fit in and belong,
So think before you act don't treat him so wrong.

Prejudice because of one's sexual orientation, how they look, their views on things, etc., is just wrong. If you have nothing good to say to or about someone then please just leave them alone.

Losing Love

I've felt the loss of losing love
When I was young I was just like you.
It's hard and your heart feels broken,
Seems there's nothing you can do.

Please think things through before you act.
Take some time, it will help you to see
It's hard and your heart feels broken,
It's tough on you, it was tough on me.

But you have friends who care about you.
Hang with them and go have some fun.
You have parents and your family,
You are young it's your time in the sun.

And as time goes by you will realize
There's a reason things go like they do.
You'll move on and find someone that you love,
And that someone will also love you.

Almost everyone goes through this in life. There is more than one person out there in the world for you, so take some time if you have a breakup and do things to keep yourself busy until you feel better. Talk to a counselor if need be; they are people who want to help you.

Forest Hedge

Safe and secure inside the hedge,
Why would I ever - ever come out?
Expose myself to all the others,
They do not know what I'm about.

I am warm and free inside this place,
No one can hurt or bother me.
Why would I leave when I am happy?
Please let me be - please let me be.

You don't get it I'm sure, and you don't know.
How can you see what's inside of me?
I do not think - no I know it's so.
You just don't see- you just don't see...

Safe and secure inside the hedge.
I feel calm it's the right place for me.
I am happy with the life that I have.
Yes I feel free - yes I feel free.

Finding out what is right for you and what makes you the happiest, in the career you choose (there are many interesting jobs), and what lifestyle you follow (social person or home body, etc.), is very important. You are your own person so do what makes you happy.

Alone

He ate his lunch there every day,
And he always ate alone.
You'd think in such a crowded place
Some kindness would be shown.

So many saw him sitting there,
You'd think someone would care.
Instead the students and the staff
Left him alone just sitting there.

It must have hurt him every time
To sit there in that place.
The cruel ones, they made fun of him.
He could see it on their face.

But he persevered and made it through,
What else could that lonely boy do?
Imagine how it would have felt,
If that lonely boy were you.

It would take courage for you to go over and invite a kid like that to come join your group for lunch, or to even sit and eat with them. But it would be a very nice thing to do, and you would make them happy.

Had It All

There was a guy that had it all,
Was so cool, was so smooth, he looked good.
But when he saw someone who was not like him,
Did his best to cut them down all he could.

But that night the fire trapped him inside,
Hard as he tried he could not get away.
Everything that he was including his pride,
Was all gone all he was burned away.

As he lay in bed full of deep despair.
Yes he knew all he'd been was all gone.
The ones who came to see him there,
Were the ones he had treated so wrong.

They knew what it's like when no one cares,
When you're not cool and you do not look right.
For him they showed their love and shared,
Helped him cope; helped him get through the night.

As popular as you may be, and you think you have everything going for you and you are invincible, all it takes is a car accident, fire, medical condition, etc., and everything changes. Be thankful and humble in life, and be good to others.

Love of the Game

You missed the shot, that's alright.
You dropped the ball, it's OK
It happens you know, to the best of them.
It happens somewhere every day.

It's a game that's why they call it a game,
Not a matter of life or of death.
If things don't go right just remember
Toughen up and just take a deep breath.

Get up off the ground and get going,
Don't look back, keep on grinding ahead.
The good ones, they have that short memory,
And the good ones look forward instead.

So never give up and keep trying.
To whine and complain does no good.
For the love of the game you should be playing,
If you're not, something's wrong and you should.

Far less than 1% of all high school athletes go on to make it to the professional level. Play because you love the sport; work hard when you train, be a good sport, and give it all you got when you compete.

In The Mirror

You are smart and you sure are sneaky
Behind their backs you always get away.
Makes you feel pretty cool when you do it.
I'm hoping for you that that feeling goes away.

You are letting down those who care about you.
And in your heart you know that it's not right.
If you're a good person and you have a conscience,
When you lay in bed it bothers you late at night.

You have no idea how much that they love you.
Until you're a parent, you haven't been there.
Some day you may see, but right now you don't know.
You have no idea just how much they really care.

So my hope for you is that you listen.
Just wanted to share this between you and me...
At the end of it all you have to answer
To the person in the mirror that you see.

Nobody can force you to be a good person and to do what is right.
You can choose to be a sneaky person and get away with things that
you know you shouldn't be doing; or you can choose to be a good and
honest person. You will be much happier if you are good and honest.

Never Gave Up

He took to the mat match after match,
Wrestling JV throughout his senior year.
And he lost each match time after time,
The thought of losing he never did fear.

I admired him and I couldn't figure out
What drove him to wrestle even though he knew,
That he'd do his best leave it all on the mat,
But on the losing end he'd be when the match was through.

Then one night our varsity guy went home sick.
Wrestle varsity against our rival, Denny had to go.
The team hoped at the best that he wouldn't get pinned,
He could save us 3 points we all hoped it was so.

So he took the mat like the man that he was,
He wrestled hard back and forth the match went.
And when it was all over the ref raised his hand
Because of Denny to us victory went.

I've run into that man and each time that I do
Our conversation goes back with delight.
Never once have we spoken of the matches he lost.
What comes up was he was a hero that night.

This is a true story about one of my former wrestlers from the Wautoma Wrestling Team in Central Wisconsin. Remember that everyone that is on a team is important no matter how good they are. Practicing hard, doing your best, and being a good sport are the keys. And don't forget about team managers and other people who are behind the scenes; they are important also.

What Honor Have You?

If you lie and cheat to hurt someone
I ask this question - what honor have you?
If you need to do that to succeed,
I think it's time for you to think things through.

Because if you keep on doing what you do
Years will go by and you'll still be there.
When you look back and think about your life,
You'll feel the guilt that you'll have to bear.

You'll know you hurt people you shouldn't have hurt,
Because you did things that you know were wrong.
And you'll never be able to change that fact,
Can't change the lyrics of your lousy song.

So if you're doing some things you shouldn't do
And you want to make what's wrong so it's right,
Then you'd better change what you are doing in life.
I think you'll be able to sleep better at night.

If you are living your life dishonestly and you don't change, someday you'll look back and realize what you have done; and by then it will be too late to make the wrongs you've done right.

The Rainbow

There is gold at the end of the rainbow,
Open your eyes you'll be able to see.
Yes there's gold at the end of the rainbow,
And it's waiting for you to set you free.

You just have to find what you're looking for.
That niche in life that is perfect for you.
Go after the thing that suites you best.
You'll be happy when you find what's for you.

It doesn't matter what the other people say,
It's your life you can do as you please.
Find your passion and then just go for it.
Listen to yourself, you will be more at ease.

You'll find your dreams and get what you want,
You will enjoy doing the thing that fits you.
You'll be happy because within your heart,
You will know you are living your life true.

Find out what your true passion in life is, and then work toward getting a job in that area. You may have to go to college or technical school and study hard; but it will be worth it in the long run. The military is also a great option for those that like or need discipline.

Addiction

Ever since you can remember it's always been a part of you
Even though you know it's wrong something you always had to do
The battle that never goes away it goes on and on each day
A force too strong you can't defeat you figure it's here to stay

Then one day you make a battle plan you decide you've had enough
Prepare to fight an enemy that to this point has been too tough
You give it all you've got but this foe refuses to be beat
You thought you had a winning plan but this time you taste defeat

Time goes on and you regroup there has to be another way
You must defeat this nemesis you must drive it far away
Then you try again you give your all but it's unwilling to retreat
Despite a valiant effort again you go down in bitter defeat

You drag yourself up off the ground try to mount a charge again
To give up now not an option you know that would surely mean the end
The harder you fight you realize the more forces this enemy sends
You try to fight on through until the wounds inside you mend

This enemy knows when you are weak and it knows when you are strong
It knows when you want to choose what's right and when you're ready to do wrong
How do you fight something that seems to know what you will do?
How do you beat this thing when you find that the foe you are fighting is you?

In time you begin to realize that you can't beat this thing alone
So many times you've battled it but defeat is all you've known
If you're smart and in your heart this war you really want to win
Then you'll face the fact to beat it you need others to begin

To help you see what you need to see and what you have to do
To help to fight this battle and to help to push you through
Help to face this foe and beat this force and then destroy it too
Help break down the wall and conquer it and free the real you

Then you will find another life and you will finally be free
To do the things you want to do and then be able to see
That the enemy that held you captive now unable to hurt you
You'll feel freedom in your heart and your mind will be free too

All but three of the following stories are examples of young people who unfortunately never got the opportunity that you have in front of you right now. They would trade places with you in a heartbeat for the chance to live a long and fulfilling life. If you are wasting the gift you have been given, it is a dishonor to them; so please think about that as you read through each story.

Their Eagle Now Soars

Their Eagle now soars in the brightness above,
Watching down on the ones that he loves.
They loved him too, of that Aaron was sure.
Unconditional love for him solid and pure.

It's apparent to me though I didn't know this kid.
He did his best despite the physical troubles he had.
Accomplished so much in a short time, he sure did.
Thoughts of his life make me happy...yet also sad.

He could have given up early and said woe is me,
Waste the 30 years he was given in this life.
Something inside gave him the strength to see,
And his family and friends helped him fight through the strife.

Take a lesson from Aaron and the life that he lived.
Don't waste the time you've been given, don't you see?
Take a lesson from Aaron for time to him was a gift.
Make the best of your life, that's the way it should be.

Aaron was born in Oshkosh, Wisconsin, and at the age of 2 he was diagnosed with a terminal illness. Despite all the physical struggles he endured, Aaron, with the help of family and friends, accomplished more in his 30 years of life than many people do in a full lifetime.

Her Spot

She took her spot on the gym floor,
On what would be her last full day.
She laughed and played and had her fun,
And then she went away.

To read about the fire then
It made my heart just sink.
I thought about that little girl,
It really made me think.

Life can be short, life can be long;
That's just the way it goes.
The reason that it is that way
There is only one that knows.

But if our lives were all the same
And we never saw the strife,
How would we then appreciate
This gift that is our life.

A little 1st grade student of mine who came to physical education class on a Friday and died in a fire with her older sister the following night.

All American

He was an All American.
He was young and proud with no fear.
He went to protect what he believed,
In a land far away from us here.

What made him go and leave his home?
Go to a place so different and far away?
If he wasn't an All American,
He could have stayed taken the easy way.

But he felt that call to duty,
Wanted to serve so we all would be free.
And those that knew him they were sure,
A fine soldier he surely would be.

But one day this fine young soldier
Protecting what he believed and loved,
In the wrong place at the wrong time,
Now All American stands guard from above.

A brave soldier from East Central Wisconsin who gave his life for our country.

Johnny

We didn't understand it back then,
When we heard that Johnny went away.
It hit us hard but only when
We saw him pale and cold that sad day.

Why was it him and why not me?
Between my 7th and 8th grade years.
So many times I've tried to see,
There are times it has brought me to tears.

Just a normal kid like everyone.
He rode his bike to go fishing that day,
But in a short time his life was done.
His heart failed and he passed away.

Why was it him and why not me?
Forty plus years he's been gone, I'm still here.
I've tried to understand and see,
But there's no reason so nothing is clear.

Our 7th grade flag football quarterback who was my classmate and good friend. He had an unknown heart defect and he died in the summer before 8th grade started.

Marty

He woke that day and never dreamed
That this would be the end.
They asked the men for volunteers,
And he was one that went.

To save the child that was inside,
He never blinked an eye.
And as he tried to save that kid
Our good friend Marty died.

And Marty's dad he blamed himself
Because the son he loved was gone.
For he had got Marty that job,
Then everything went wrong.

Although his son was hailed a hero
For what he did that day
His father's mind could not be changed,
To look at it that way.

A great guy and friend from Evanston, Illinois. Marty was a firefighter/paramedic who died when he was 27 years old trying to save a one-month-old baby during a fire. He had volunteered to go into the burning building to search for the child that day.

Memorial Day

The flags fly low Memorial Day
To honor those that died.
But all you think of is your son,
How many times you've cried.

For he was one who gave his life
So we could all be free.
But every day you ask yourself,
Why did this have to be?

There must have been a reason
For God to take this fine young man.
You may not understand it,
Rest assured it's in His plan.

And when your days are over
You will go where he has been.
The tears you've cried forever dried,
You'll understand it then.

This is about the same brave soldier from East Central Wisconsin. I stopped and wrote this about him and his mother on Memorial Day when I drove through his hometown of Omro. There were flags flying on both sides of Main Street on a brilliant cloudless day.

So Young

She lies in bed so young so new,
So scared and so alone.
There's nothing they can do for her,
And she just wants to go home.

How fair is life to this sweet girl,
When it starts and then it's done.
I'd like to know—please tell me how,
This happens to one so young.

No high school prom or college days,
No thrill of that first kiss.
How fair is this to one so pure,
All the fun in life she'll miss

But I trust that God has made a place
Where she'll play, she'll laugh, she'll be loved.
To give her what she's lost down here,
Yes, I believe it's there above.

Such a sad thing that happens far too many times.
My beliefs and hopes are in this story.

Their Angel

Two days ago—please say it isn't so,
Their world stopped turning; they got the word.
Two days ago—please say it isn't so.
Their world stopped turning when they heard.

Their Angel that they loved so much,
The one who made them smile,
Had flown on to a better place,
They only had her for a while.

She's gone on to a higher place
To watch them from above.
And with her she took all her grace,
To a place with only love.

Because they believe He died for us
So that we could all be free,
Their Angel that they love so much,
Someday they all will see.

*A mother I know lost her beautiful teenage daughter
in a car accident.*

War

Young men were dying everywhere,
There was chaos all around.
Some turned and tried to run away,
Some lie trembling on the ground.

Young men were dying everywhere.
They were so young, it wasn't fair.
Some lucky ones got away and lived.
Some young lives just ended right there.

How can it be in those foreign lands,
That some lived, while other boys died.
Some survived, went on to live long lives.
Some lives stopped, mothers and fathers cried.

No rhyme or reason to it all,
We can't begin to figure out why
Some were chosen to live out their lives,
Some, sad to say, were just destined to die.

Appreciate the life and freedom that you have been given.
Great sacrifices were given and many lives were lost to
allow you the chance you have to live a long, meaningful,
and happy life.

Soldier of God

As he grew up he never dreamed
That he'd be in this place.
It went against what he was taught,
This thing that he now faced.

To make the choice of kill or die
Was what he had to do.
It's you get him and if you don't,
Then surely he'll get you.

How could he do what must be done
To make it home alive?
Whatever way the young man chose
His heart would not survive.

So in the end he made the choice,
The only one he could.
The choice he made—it was the one
The Bible said he should.

His gun went down, his hands went up,
And quickly it was done.
He did the thing that he believed,
And met his Chosen One.

Young men in World Wars 1 and 2 had no choice, and had to go to war. Some of them, because of their religious beliefs, fear, or other personal feelings, could not kill another human being, and thus made the ultimate sacrifice.

Hero

The battle raged, carnage all around.
Everywhere he looked men were going down.
Soldiers were hit, what should he do?
Should he leave them there or see it through?

He had the choice—move ahead or run.
It's likely no one would ever know.
He could stay and help his brothers,
Or turn his back on them and go.

Turn and run away to save himself,
Make that choice and most likely he'd live.
Move ahead and help his comrades,
And a good chance his life he would give.

Nobody would ever know or see
What choice this soldier made.
But he ran anyway into the fight instead,
He made that choice and stayed.

And he never made it out of there.
But for a while he helped all he could.
No one ever knew what he had done,
For this unknown hero I wish they would.

This happened many times in war. Many sacrifices have been made so you can live a life of freedom in our country.

Tommy Boy

The stone said Tommy and that was all,
No date of birth or death.
It never said when he was born,
Or the date of his last breath.

I tried to picture Tommy Boy,
How he laughed and how he cried.
Was he happy with the life he had?
And what happened, how he died?

He did not have the silver spoon,
And I know that he was poor,
Judging by his simple stone,
His family needed more.

And did he have the brain to make
A difference in his world.
If given time to use that gift,
Before his life unfurled.

Or was his life tough from the start,
A life that wasn't fair?
Was he given love from Mom and Dad?
Or did neither of them care?

How short was his time on this earth?
How come it doesn't say?
I guess for this forgotten boy
It's meant to stay that way.

A flat gravestone I saw in a cemetery in Oshkosh, Wisconsin.
TOMMY never got a chance to live a long life to fulfill his destiny.
Take advantage of the time you have.

For the Parent

Comes a time they seem to forget about us,
All grown up they live how they want to live.
Hard as you try there's nothing we can do.
Give their time to those they want to give it to.

We have to face the fact those days are done.
When they were ours for just you and for me.
Night and day they were our moon and sun,
Those days are gone now we have to let it be.

Once upon a time it seems so long ago,
Those special days they were so good.
Oh yes we sure do wish it still were so,
If we could relive it yes surely we would.

Let's just be happy now for what we had.
We were quite lucky you know it's true.
Let's try to be happy—turn away from the sad.
God smiled very well upon me and you.

TO THE YOUNGER: As you get older, try to remember those that raised you and took care of you as you were growing up. It's easy to spend all your time having fun with your friends; but try to take a little time and reach out to those that were there for you when you were young. Remember they were there when you needed them.

It's a Parent's War Too

Day after day you worry about him,
Just like you did when he was young.
Yes day after day you worry about him,
But too far away nothing can be done.

The days so long seem to last forever,
But the nights are much longer you realize.
The worry and fear that the word may come,
Those endless nights hard to close your eyes.

They want to kill your son and you know it.
He's a main target, yes it's sad to say.
You lie awake you know each coming day
Might be the day that he's taken away.

And day after day you pray to God above,
To protect him and bring him back to you.
And after each day you're one day closer,
One day closer to that dream coming true.

If you're lucky the day comes you hold him in your arms.
Yes he's a man but he'll always be your boy.
Finally home for good you thank the Lord above.
Endless nights replaced with endless joy.

A friend of mine expressed the scope of worry that he and his wife had about their son Matt while he was serving in Iraq.

TO THE YOUNGER: No matter what your home situation is, those that raised you probably care and worry about you way more than you think; and in many cases, they care about you more than they care about themselves.

Courage

Aboard that ship or in the field,
On that aircraft, in that tank.
To risk your life the way you did,
Every one of you I thank.

How did you do the things you did,
Knowing the end was always near?
How did you handle all those thoughts,
And deal with all that fear?

To those that served and didn't return
I know this much is true:
You'll never be forgotten,
And my hat goes off to you.

And lest we not forget the ones,
For the wounded—you eased their pain.
To see and do the things you did,
The horror and the strain.

To you that made it back alive,
For some it must be tough.
How hard it has to be some days
To remember all that stuff.

For even though you made it back,
Some pain I'm sure you've hid.
True heroes every one of you,
For everything you did.

Many Americans made great sacrifices in wars to bring you the freedom that you have; and many gave their lives for your freedom. Please remember that, and honor them by living a good and meaningful life.

TO THE YOUNGER: The military is a great career and great option if you need discipline and want to get your life on the right track.

www.ingramcontent.com/pod-product-compliance
Lightning Source LLC
Chambersburg PA
CBHW060041040426
42331CB00032B/1987